Creatures of the Dark

CONTENTS

A World of Darkness

At the end of each day, when darkness falls, many creatures are just waking up. These creatures are *nocturnal* animals. They are active at night, and they sleep during the day.

Other creatures live in places that are dark all the time, such as deep caves, or the bottom of the ocean.

Raccoons
Loris

Seeing in the Dark

Eyes need light to work. Humans can see well when there is plenty of light. But many nocturnal animals can see well when there is very little light.

Many nocturnal animals, like this mouse lemur, have very large eyes.

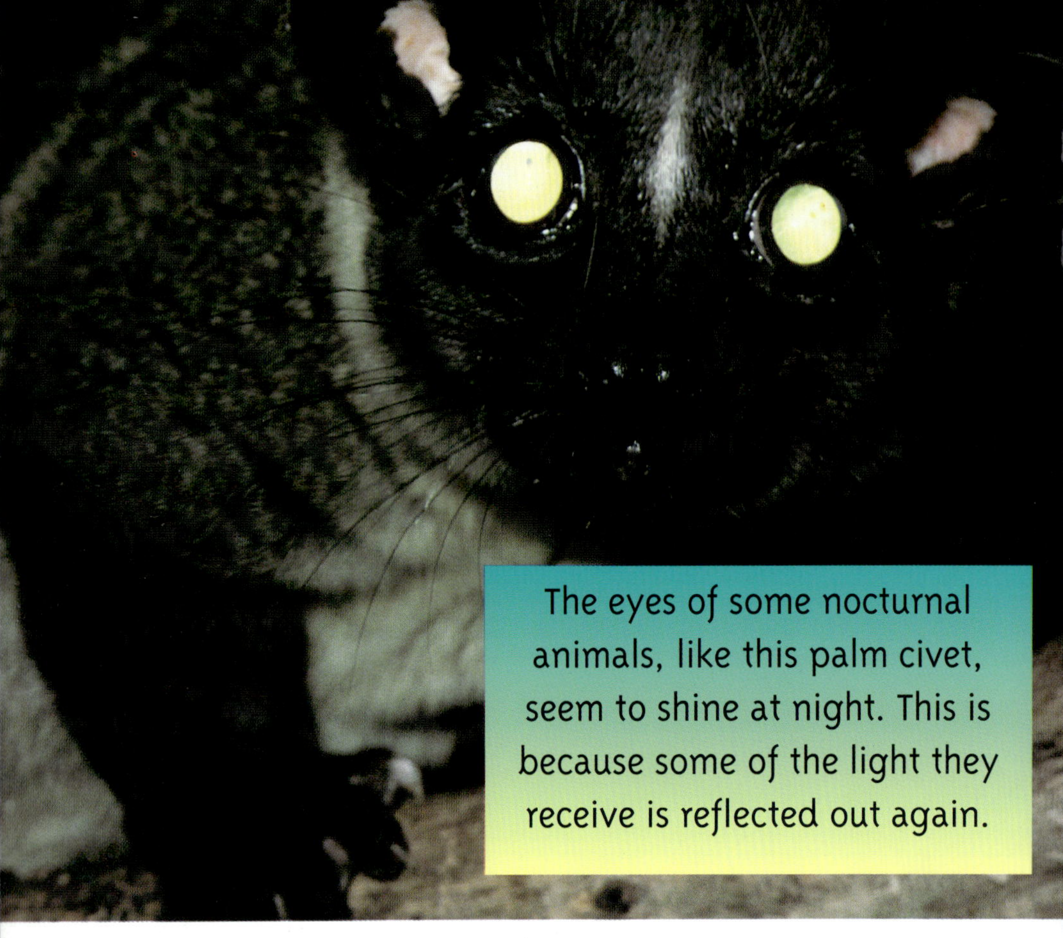

Many nocturnal animals have a kind of mirror in their eyes, known as a *tapetum*. The tapetum reflects the light that the eyes receive; this makes the light seem stronger and helps the animal to see.

Some animals that are active at night also come out in the daytime. Their eyes need to be able to adjust to different amounts of light.

The pupil (the dark central part of the eye) lets in the light. Cats' pupils become narrow slits in daylight. In the dark, they open wide to let in as much light as possible.

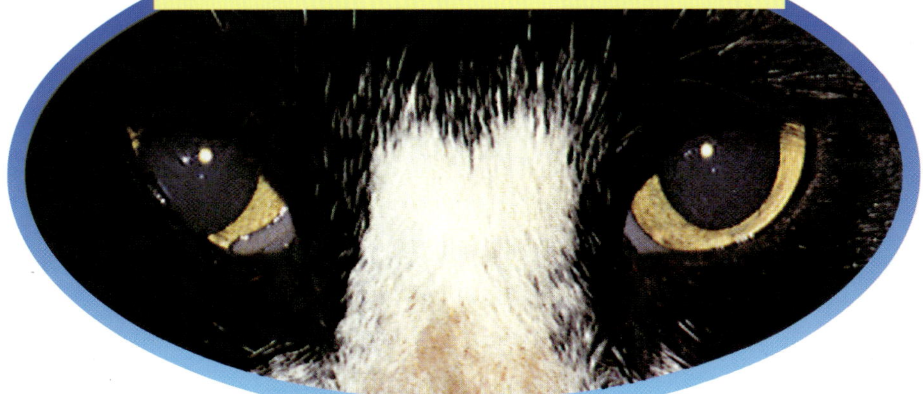

Sounds in the Dark

In the dark, many creatures rely on their sense of hearing to help them move around safely. Many nocturnal animals can hear very faint sounds – even a leaf falling.

Large ears help the fennec fox to hear faint, night sounds.

Barn owls use hearing
as well as sight to
find their food.

Flying Blind

Bats are almost completely blind. They use sounds to find their way and to hunt for their food.

Bats make very *high-pitched* sounds – too high for people to hear. These sounds bounce off objects and produce echoes. A bat can tell where an object is by listening to the echo that travels back. This process is called *echolocation*.

Bats sleep during
the day, hanging
upside down
in trees or caves.

Safety in the Dark

For many creatures, the dark night is the safest time to be out and about.

Some flightless birds, such as kiwis, spend the day in burrows and come out at night to look for food.

Elephant hawk moth

Some moths are nocturnal. They rest
during the day, hiding from hunters
such as spiders and birds. At night they
go in search of flowers and their nectar.

But the night is not completely safe.
Moths must always be listening for bats.
When moths sense bats approaching, they
stop flying and drop straight to the ground.

Escaping the Heat

Deserts can be burning hot during the day. Some desert animals avoid the hot sun by coming out only at night.

Grasshopper mice come out of their burrows at night. They howl outside the burrow to scare other animals.

At night, deserts can be very cold. Many nocturnal animals, such as sandcats, have thick coats to keep them warm.
Gerbils come out at night to collect water from seeds covered with dew.

Caves and Burrows

Some creatures live in darkness all the time.

Moles spend their lives in dark tunnels. They are almost completely blind, and depend on the senses of touch and smell.

Glowworms produce
a faint light. This
attracts small insects
that the glowworms
catch and eat.

Underwater Darkness

The deepest parts of the oceans are dark all the time. Many underwater caves are completely dark, too.

Many creatures that live in this darkness are blind. They find their way around rocks and other obstacles by "feeling" slight changes in water pressure.

Cave-dwelling fish have no eyes.

Angler fish produce
tiny amounts of light to
attract their food.

In the Garden

Some garden creatures are active at night.

Snails usually hide in dark, damp places during the day so that they won't dry out. They come out at night or after rain to eat plants.

Many insects are active after the sun goes down. Garden spiders mend their webs each evening so that they will be ready to catch insects during the night.

Catching a Glimpse

Some zoos have special areas for displaying nocturnal animals. These areas have bright lights on at night, so that the nocturnal animals go to sleep. Then, during the day, the displays are lit with very dim light; the animals think that it is night and become active.

Scientists use a special kind of light,
called *infrared* light, for watching nocturnal
animals. We can't see infrared light, but it
can be used to produce pictures that we
can see.

GLOSSARY

echoes - sounds that bounce off objects and travel back to where they came from

echolocation - a process of using echoes to locate objects

infrared light - a kind of light that is invisible to humans. Infrared light is given off by living things and can be used to produce pictures in the dark.

nocturnal animals - animals that are active during the night and sleep during the day

pupil - part of the eye that lets in light

tapetum - a kind of mirror inside the eyes of some nocturnal animals. The tapetum reflects light, helping the animal to see when there is little light.

INDEX